Living on an Island

Richard Spilsbury

www.heinemannlibrary.co.uk

Visit our website to find out more information about Heinemann Library books.

To order:

☎ Phone +44 (0) 1865 888066
🖷 Fax +44 (0) 1865 314091
🖳 Visit www.heinemannlibrary.co.uk

Heinemann Library is an imprint of Capstone Global Library Limited, a company incorporated in England and Wales having its registered office at 7 Pilgrim Street, London, EC4V 6LB - Registered company number: 6695582

"Heinemann" is a registered trademark of Pearson Education Limited, under licence to Capstone Global Library Limited.

Text © Capstone Global Library Limited 2010
First published in hardback in 2010
The moral rights of the proprietor have been asserted.

Edited by Charlotte Guillain and
  Catherine Veitch
Designed by Joanna Hinton-Malivoire
Original illustrations © Capstone Global Library
Illustrated by Joanna Hinton-Malivoire
Picture research by Elizabeth Alexander and
  Fiona Orbell
Originated by Dot Gradations Ltd
Printed in China by South China Printing Company Ltd

ISBN 978 0 431020 90 7 (hardback)
14 13 12 11 10
10 9 8 7 6 5 4 3 2 1

British Library Cataloguing in Publication Data
Spilsbury, Richard
Living on an island. – (Our local area)
910.9'142-dc22
A full catalogue record for this book is available from the British Library.

Acknowledgements

We would like to thank the following for permission to reproduce photographs: Alamy pp. **8** (© Robert Harding Picture Library Ltd.), **11** (© Neil McAllister), **15** (© David Davies), **18** (© Ashley Cooper), **19** (© Imagespace); © British International p. **9**; Corbis pp. **4** & **5** (© Jason Hawkes), **6** (© Skyscan), **10** (© Ashley Cooper), **12** (© Sergio Pitamitz), **17** (© Patrick Ward), **20** & **21** (© Fridmar Damm/Zefa); Getty Images p. **14** (F.J. Mortimer/Hulton Archive); © Nic Slocum p. **8**; Science Photo Library p. **7** (Planetary Visions Ltd.).

Cover photograph of St. Aubins Harbour, Channel Islands, Jersey, United Kingdom reproduced with permission of Alamy (© Jon Arnold Images Ltd).

We would like to thank Rachel Bowles for her invaluable help in the preparation of this book.

Contents

Any words appearing in the text in bold, **like this**, are explained in the glossary.

Water all around

Islands are land completely surrounded by water. Some islands are in the middle of lakes or rivers. Ocean islands have seawater all around them.

Some islands were made by **volcanoes** under the sea. Hot melted rock from the volcano hardened as it cooled, forming an island. Some islands are areas of land that have become separated from the **mainland** by rising water.

Think of three ways this island is like where you live, and three ways in which it is different.

Island life

Some islands are too small and rocky for people to live on. Seabirds such as cormorants and gulls may fly to the islands to build their nests and lay eggs. Other islands are big enough to have several towns and villages, for example the Isle of Man and Isle of Wight.

Bass Rock in Scotland is mostly home to ganet seabirds.

This is a photo of Great Britain at night. You can see the shape of the island because of all the lights. Where do you think most people live?

Great Britain is a big island. There is space for tens of millions of people to live on the **mainland**. Look on a globe or in an **atlas** to see the British Isles. How many groups of islands can you count apart from Great Britain? Have you been to any of these islands?

Getting on and off islands

Some islands are connected to the **mainland** by a bridge or tunnel. People can drive over the water on a bridge, or under the water through a tunnel, to get to the island. Some islands are joined to the mainland by a beach that is covered with seawater when the **tide** comes in.

When the tide goes out, you can walk to this island on a raised path called a **causeway**.

People may have to travel by ferry boat to
get to islands that are further away. Some
ferry boats are big enough to carry cars and
lorries, too. You can also fly over the water in
helicopters and planes that land on islands.
This is how people reach the Outer Hebrides,
Orkneys, and Shetland Isles near Scotland.

What's on an island?

An island is made up of many natural **features**. All islands have a coast where the land meets the sea. A coast is made up of **cliffs**, beaches, and rocks. Inland, other natural features include hills, **moors**, land with fields, rivers, and lakes.

The cliffs on this island were formed when the sea wore away rock from the hills.

Can you label the lighthouse and jetty on this island?

Other things on an island are made by people, such as houses and outbuildings to provide shelter and workplaces. There is usually a **lighthouse** to warn ships away from dangerous rocks by the coast. There is a **jetty** where boats can stop to load and unload.

An island map

We can use maps to find our way around an island. Maps are flat pictures that show a bird's eye view of a place. They show us what an area looks like from above.

Compare this photo of an island from above with the map of the same island opposite.

Maps use symbols to show us where things are. Symbols are letters or pictures that represent different things. A **key** tells us what the symbols mean.

> Can you use the key and map to find out where the church is? Are there any campsites on the island?

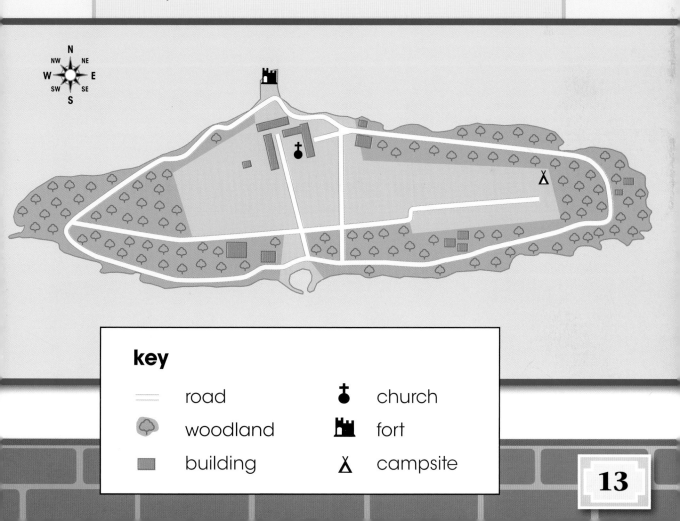

key

───	road	♟	church
🌳	woodland	🏰	fort
▬	building	⛺	campsite

Island people

In the past, most island people worked on the land or the sea. Some caught fish in the water around the island from fishing boats. Others grew **crops** on the land, or kept animals for milk and meat. Others made cloth out of wool from island sheep.

There used to be hundreds of fishing boats on the Scilly Isles.

This islander takes visitors for rides in a horse and cart.

Today, some people are farmers or fishermen, but there are many other jobs, too. Some islanders look after the people who visit for holidays. They run hotels, look after holiday cottages, cook food in restaurants, or work in **museums**.

Visitors

Some people visit islands to explore the countryside. They come to see the birds and other animals, such as deer or seals, that live on the island or in the water around the island. Some people come to enjoy the beaches around the island coast.

People take boat trips off the island of Mull in Scotland to see whales.

People also visit the shops, tearooms, and **museums** on an island. They visit castles and other old buildings to learn about an island's past. Do you have any photos from when you visited an island? What did you like to do best?

Many people visit Lindisfarne Castle on Holy Island. The castle is over four hundred years old.

On the mainland

Some people who live on a small island travel to the **mainland** every day. Children may go to the mainland to go to school if there is not one on their island. Adults may go to the mainland to work.

The postman loads post onto the ferry on Seil Island to take it to Luing Island, in Scotland.

People use a crane to lift heavy goods from the boat onto the island **jetty**.

Many of the goods in island shops come from the mainland in lorries. The lorries bring all sorts of things, from tins of food to newspapers and books. However, islanders may also visit the mainland to visit bigger shops that sell a wider variety of goods, such as computers or musical instruments.

World of islands

There are different kinds of islands around the world. Some islands are huge. Australia is an enormous island where millions of people live. New Zealand has two main islands. How many large islands can you see in an **atlas** map of Japan?

Holidaymakers may take trips far away from home to tropical islands where they can sunbathe and swim in the warm water every day.

Some islands are rocky and very cold. Greenland is an **Arctic** island mostly covered with ice. In warm, **tropical** parts of the world there are islands with palm trees and white sandy beaches. How are these islands the same or different to islands you have visited or read about?

Island challenge

A fisherman has lost his nets on this island. You can use the **compass** to help him find them. You arrive by ferry at Jutsons' Landing. You walk north-west to buy lunch from a village. The nets are in the building to the south of the **lighthouse**. What is the building and what natural **feature** did you go through on the way?

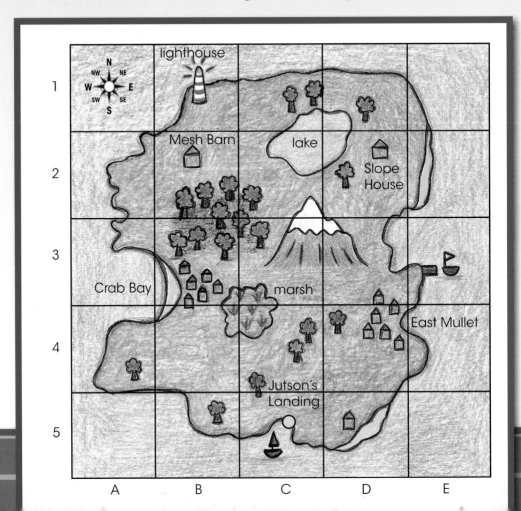

Glossary

Arctic cold region around the North Pole

atlas book containing maps and information about the world

causeway raised path across low or wet ground

cliff wide, steep rock face bordering lower land or sea

compass device to find directions

crop plants people grow for food or for other uses

features the characteristics or appearance of an object or person

jetty structure built over the sea for boats to land at and to help protect the coastline

key list of words explaining what symbols mean

lighthouse tower or other building beside the sea with a powerful light to warn or guide ships at sea

mainland main part of land making up a country

moors open land with peat soil and heather or bracken plants

museum building in which people collect, study, and look after rare or interesting objects for other people to see

tide regular rise and fall of the height of the sea. Tides are caused by the Moon moving around the Earth.

tropical warm, rainy region of Earth around the middle of the planet

volcano hole in the Earth's surface, often in a mountain, through which hot rock and gas escape

23

Index

Find out more

Books to read

An Island Home (SuperSchemes Unit 03), Liz Lewis
(Geographical Association, 2005)

Katie Morag titles, Mairi Hedderwick (Red Fox)

Websites

BBC Northern Ireland, Island Life
**www.bbc.co.uk/northernireland/schools/4_11/tykids/islandlife/
whatisanisland/index.shtml**

This site gives lots of island information, contrasts different islands, and
even has a "build an island" activity.